CRAYOLA CREATORS

Edwin Binney and C. Harold Smith

LEE SLATER

**Checkerboard
Library**

An Imprint of Abdo Publishing
abdopublishing.com

abdopublishing.com

Printed in the United States of America, North Mankato, Minnesota
102015
012016

THIS BOOK CONTAINS
RECYCLED MATERIALS

Content Developer: Nancy Tuminelly
Design and Production: Mighty Media, Inc.
Series Editor: Paige Polinsky
Cover Photos: Image provided courtesy of Crayola LLC and used with permission, © 2015 Crayola (center); Mighty Media (border)
Interior Photos: AP Images, pp. 15, 22, 25, 27; Courtesy of the Library of Congress, p. 9; Courtesy of The Strong®, Rochester, New York, pp. 13, 23, 29 (top left); Evan Amos, p. 22; Shutterstock, pp. 6, 7, 11, 17, 19, 21, 28, 29; Wikimedia Commons, p. 5.

Library of Congress Cataloging-in-Publication Data
Slater, Lee, 1969-
 Crayola creators : Edwin Binney and C. Harold Smith / Lee Slater.
    p. cm. -- (Toy trailblazers)
 Includes index.
 ISBN 978-1-62403-976-8
1. Binney, Edwin--Juvenile literature. 2. Smith, C. Harold, 1860-1931--Juvenile literature. 3. Industrialists--United States--Biography--Juvenile literature. 4. Binney & Smith Co.--Juvenile literature. 5. Crayons--Juvenile literature. I. Title.
 NC870.S59 2016
 741.2'3--dc23
                    2015030429

CONTENTS

Chapter 1

All in THE FAMILY

How did a small **charcoal** business lead to one of the most successful toys ever? The **formula** was a mix of opportunity, teamwork, and color. The result was the Crayola crayon. Its creators, Harold Smith and Edwin Binney, were cousins. But the Crayola story really begins with Edwin's father, Joseph.

Joseph W. Binney was born in England on December 6, 1836. In the 1800s, many people were moving to the United States. It was known as "The Land of Opportunity." Joseph **immigrated** to the United States in 1860. Joseph's sister, Eliza, decided to stay in England. That same year, she had a son. His name was C. Harold Smith.

In 1864, Joseph founded a factory near Peekskill, New York. It was called Peekskill Chemical Works. The company packaged **hardwood** charcoal, which was used for heating fuel. It also manufactured **lampblack** from soot and whale oil. Lampblack was used in everything from ink to shoe polish.

Peekskill, New York, was one of the country's early industrial centers.

Joseph soon met and married Annie Eliza Conklin. They had eight children together. Their son Edwin was born on November 24, 1866. He attended public schools in Peekskill and New York City.

Meanwhile, C. Harold Smith spent his teenage years in New Zealand. Then, in 1878, he moved to the United States. Together, Edwin and Harold would make the world come alive with color.

Chapter 2

BINNEY & SMITH

In 1880, Joseph moved the Peekskill Chemical Works's headquarters to New York City. He hired his nephew Harold as a salesman. Soon after, Edwin joined the company as a salesman too. Besides **charcoal** and **lampblack**, Peekskill Chemical Works made paint with red **iron oxide**. Joseph taught Harold and Edwin everything about the business. They learned about color **pigments,** manufacturing, marketing, and sales.

Edwin and Harold worked well together. They were looking for new ways to grow the business. When Joseph retired in 1885, they took a new direction. They changed

Farmers often bought Peekskill Chemical Works' red paint for their barns.

the company's name to Binney & Smith.

The next year, Edwin married Alice Stead in Brooklyn, New York. They had four children, three girls and a boy. Harold married Paula Smith. Together they had a boy and a girl.

In the 1890s, the company created a new **pigment** called carbon black. Carbon black was much darker than **lampblack**. It was used in dyes, paint, printing ink, and shoe polish. One of the main ingredients in carbon black was oil. Oil had been discovered in Pennsylvania in the 1850s. So, the company had a local source for **raw material**.

Binney developed new products and expanded sales in the United States. Smith traveled all over the world to find new markets for their products. Thanks to the cousins' **complementary** skills and efforts, the company **thrived**. Binney and Smith made a great team!

Chapter 3

A Brand-New MARKET

Binney was always working to find new uses for carbon black. By mixing it with certain waxes, Binney & Smith created a black crayon marker. The marker was used to write on crates and barrels. The product was called Staonal, a combination of the words "stay on all." The crayon was wrapped in paper so the carbon would not stain the workers' hands.

Binney's wife, Alice, inspired another new product. Alice was a schoolteacher, and her students used pencils for everything. The pencils had square leads made from clay, slate, and **graphite**. Binney developed a better pencil using local slate.

In 1900, Binney & Smith moved to Easton, Pennsylvania, to be closer to the slate mines. This reduced the expense of transporting the company's **raw materials**. The company also bought a water-powered stone mill to grind the slate.

In the 1800s, Pennsylvania was one of the world's largest slate producers.

Teachers and students loved the new pencils. There were schools all over the country. And all the students needed pencils. This new market offered great opportunity!

Chapter 4

The Art of LISTENING

As Smith traveled the country selling pencils, he listened to schoolteachers. He asked what other educational supplies they needed. Many teachers told him that they had a problem with chalk. It created a lot of dust whenever they wrote on the blackboard.

Smith brought the news back to the company. Binney immediately began experimenting with new ways to make chalk. In 1902, the company introduced An-Du-Septic Blackboard Chalk. It was the first dustless chalk, and schools eagerly bought the product.

Smith continued to listen carefully to the teachers he met. It seemed that teachers everywhere wanted safe, inexpensive coloring supplies. Most professional coloring supplies

FUN FACT

An-Du-Septic Blackboard Chalk won a gold medal at the 1904 St. Louis World's Fair.

Binney and Smith's new dustless chalk was very popular among teachers.

were full of toxic chemicals. They were much too dangerous for children. Colored crayons were **available**, but they had to be imported from Europe. They were expensive, and the quality was poor. Smith told Binney what the teachers wanted. And Binney saw another great opportunity.

Chapter 5

THE CRAYOLA
Crayon Is Born

The company got to work testing different ingredients and color **pigments**. In 1903, they were satisfied with the result. But Binney and Smith needed a **unique** name for these new crayons.

Luckily, Alice had another inspiration. *Craie* is the French word for chalk. *Ola* comes from the word **oleaginous** (oh-lee-AH-juh-nuhs). Alice combined the two and formed the completely original word *Crayola*. It was easy to pronounce and easy to remember. The product still goes by this name today!

The crayons were made of non-toxic materials. Waxes, **talc**, and pigments were mixed in small batches. The mixture was poured into molds where it hardened. Then workers attached paper labels to the crayons by hand.

FUN FACT

The Crayola **brand** name is recognized by more than 98 percent of American people.

In 1903, Binney and Smith introduced their first box of crayons. It included red, orange, yellow, green, blue, violet, brown, and black crayons. Best of all, they were safe for children to use.

The original Crayola crayons only cost a nickel per box!

Chapter 6

Life of A CRAYON

Uncolored **paraffin** wax arrives at the factory in heated train cars. The wax must be kept at 135 degrees Fahrenheit (57°C) to remain liquid. Workers pump the wax into tanks outside the factory. On a **typical** day, the factory uses more than 17,000 gallons (64,352 L) of wax.

The wax is pumped through pipes into large, heated mixing kettles. Workers add ingredients to help blend and strengthen the wax. Powdered **pigment** is then added to the mixture. The pigment is worked into the wax until it is evenly blended. Each kettle holds a single color.

Next, the wax mixture is pumped through pipes into crayon-shaped steel molds. As the molds are cooled with water, the crayons harden. In four to seven minutes, the crayons become solid. Light colors harden faster than dark colors.

The crayons are released from the mold at the **ejection** station. Inspectors check the crayons for **imperfections**. If a crayon is broken,

A machine helps workers sort and package the crayons.

chipped, or bubbly, it is removed from production. A robotic arm delivers acceptable crayons to the labeling area.

Machines apply labels to the crayons and roll them off the **assembly line**. The entire batch is then boxed. Each box contains crayons of one color. The boxes are then moved to the **inventory** area.

Workers package the crayons by feeding them into large funnels. One crayon of each color drops from its funnel onto a platform. A robotic arm then sweeps the crayons into the retail box.

The filled boxes are bundled together by a packing machine. Finally, they are put on pallets. The crayons are then ready to be shipped.

Chapter 7

Binney & Smith
ON THE ROAD

Binney and Smith continued to respond to consumer needs. In the early 1900s, automobiles made in the United States were new on the market. Most people traveled by train or electric streetcar. But personal transportation was a new and welcome idea.

All car manufacturers had to purchase rubber tires. At first, these tires where white. But there was a gray tire made in England. This tire was made with carbon and was extra strong. Binney & Smith had been making black carbon for years. It was the perfect resource for tire manufacturers.

In 1911, Binney and Smith received their biggest order yet. The B. F. Goodrich Company needed 1 million pounds of carbon! By adding more carbon to its rubber mixture, B. F. Goodrich created the strongest tires ever. Black tires soon became the **industry standard**.

Modern tires
are strong
and durable,
thanks to
carbon.

Chapter 8

A Great PARTNERSHIP

Binney and Smith worked together very well. They even took turns being president and vice president of the company! Their success was the product of a great partnership.

Each man had **unique** skills that **complemented** the other. Smith was an outgoing salesman. He loved to meet new people and see new places. And he was an excellent listener. He was also very good at identifying products that would meet consumer needs.

Binney was a careful businessman. He was good at developing the products Smith suggested. He worked with the chemists and designers at the factory. And he brought the products Smith **envisioned** to the market. Binney also handled

FUN FACT

Crayola produces about 3 billion crayons a year. If the crayons were placed end to end, they would circle the earth six times!

Binney and Smith's teamwork made the world a brighter place.

the company's finances. He liked quiet jobs he could do in the office.

If Binney and Smith had not worked together, there would be no Crayola today. The partnership they shared was rare in the business world.

Chapter 9

Making A DIFFERENCE

Binney and Smith became very wealthy. But they were more than great businessmen. Smith was a world traveler. He took notes about the places he visited and the people he met. In later years, he used these notes in his writing. He wrote an **autobiography**, as well as fiction books.

Binney was happy to share his wealth by contributing to his community. He **donated** money to build a park near his family. Binney Park was built on former swampland in Old Greenwich, Connecticut. It included various green areas and a lake.

Binney also had a home in Fort Pierce, Florida. He loved Florida and enjoyed boating, fishing, and designing boats. In 1922, Binney helped create an inlet for the town. The inlet allowed Fort Pierce to become a port city. After it opened, the town began to grow and prosper.

FUN FACT

Binney & Smith helped found the Crayon, Watercolor & Craft Institute. Its mission is to promote product safety in art materials.

Binney & Smith gave back to the community too. During the **Great Depression** of the 1930s, jobs were scarce. People didn't have enough money to buy basic **necessities**. The company hired jobless local farmers to put labels on crayons. The community never forgot this display of generosity.

Binney's inlet made it possible to ship Florida oranges directly from Fort Pierce.

Chapter 10

Crayola Keeps
ON COLORING

Smith died in 1931. Binney died three years later. During their lives, they made an **indelible** impression on the world. Their contributions to education and art continue to make life more fun.

Binney and Smith's company continued to **thrive** and grow without them. In 1998, Crayola crayons entered the National Toy Hall of Fame. Crayola delights consumers with **innovative** products to this day. Some of these include:

- 64-count crayon box with built-in sharpener

- Craft and activity kits
- Crayola markers

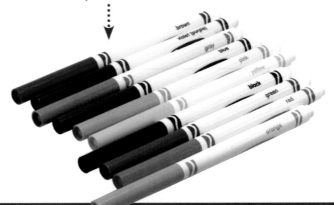

- Washable markers
- No Drip Paint Brush Pens

- Washable Sidewalk Chalk
- 96-count crayon box with built-in sharpener

Chapter 11

A CLASSIC TOY

Something that is classic has value that lasts over time. It doesn't go out of use or out of style. Crayola Crayons are definitely a classic toy. Kids have been drawing with Binney & Smith Crayola Crayons for more than 100 years. Your great-grandparents probably played with Binney & Smith crayons!

For most kids, crayons are their very first art supplies. A child's first opportunity to explore color usually starts with a crayon. In 2011, Crayola even launched a line of crayons specially designed for small hands.

Crayons continue to be a popular everyday art supply. Colorful crayon drawings dot the walls of schools everywhere. Restaurants offer placemats and crayons for children to use while they wait for their food. Crayons are affordable enough that nearly everyone has some at home.

Binney & Smith officially changed its name to Crayola in 2007. It is one of the most widely

FUN FACT

Yale University did a study on scent recognition. The study ranked crayons number 18 of the 20 scents most recognizable to American adults.

recognized **brand** names in the United States. It's also well known around
the globe. Crayola Crayons are sold in more than 80 countries. The labels
and boxes are printed in 12 different languages.

Chapter 12

A Bright, Green FUTURE

In 2001, a US poll revealed blue as the most popular crayon color. But when it comes to the **environment**, Crayola's favorite color is green! Crayola products have always been made with safe, kid-friendly ingredients.

The original business made products from carbon. Now we know that carbon is not a **renewable resource**. Today, the company is committed to reducing its **carbon footprint**. The Crayola Solar Farm uses **solar energy** to produce electricity. It creates enough electricity to produce 1 billion crayons and 500 million markers per year!

The company also focuses on reducing waste and protecting rain forests. Crayola markers are made from recycled plastic. Crayola colored pencils are produced with **reforested wood**.

In response to today's consumers, Crayola has its own line of **software**. Now kids can express their creativity with computers and tablets. The future is probably different than what Binney and Smith imagined. But both would be proud to see the Crayola business today. It continues to make the world a more colorful, beautiful place.

The Crayola ColorCycle program turns recycled markers into fuel!

TIMELINE

1860
C. Harold Smith is born.

1866
Edwin Binney is born.

1902
Binney & Smith introduces the first dustless school chalk.

1864
Joseph Binney founds Peekskill Chemical Works in upstate New York.

1885
Joseph Binney retires. Edwin Binney and C. Harold Smith form a partnership and rename Peekskill Chemical Works.

1931

C. Harold Smith dies.

1993

Binney & Smith releases a 96-count box of crayons.

1903

Binney & Smith produces the first box of eight Crayola crayons. It sells for a nickel.

1934

Edwin Binney dies.

1998

Crayola Crayons were inducted into the National Toy Hall of Fame.

Glossary

assembly line – a way of making something in which the item moves from worker to worker until it is finished.

autobiography – a story of a person's life that is written by himself or herself.

available – able to be had or used.

brand – a category of products made by a particular company and all having the same company name.

carbon footprint – the amount of pollution something releases.

charcoal – a black material that is a form of carbon.

complement – to go well with or complete something.

donate – to give.

ejection – the act of removing something from inside something else.

environment – nature and everything in it, such as the land, sea, and air.

envision – to imagine or see in one's mind.

formula – a combination of specific amounts of different ingredients or elements.

graphite – a soft, shiny, black form of carbon.

Great Depression – the period from 1929 to 1942 of worldwide economic trouble. There was little buying or selling, and many people could not find work.

hardwood – the wood from a tree that loses its leaves in the winter. Oak and maple are hardwood trees.

immigrate – to enter another country to live.

imperfection – a flaw.

indelible – impossible to erase or remove.

industry standard – a common way a type of product is made.

innovative – marked by a new idea, method, or device.

inventory – the items a business or store has in stock.

iron oxide – a compound of oxygen and iron.

lampblack – black soot used to color things black.

necessity – a thing you must have and cannot live without, such as food and shelter.

oleaginous (oh-lee-AH-juh-nuhs) – containing or producing oil.

paraffin – a type of wax often used in candles, drugs, and cosmetics.

pigment – a powder that is mixed with a liquid to create a color.

raw material – something that can be used to make a product.

reforested wood – wood from a forest that was renewed by planting seeds or young trees.

renewable resource – a resource that is capable of being replaced naturally. Renewable resources include wind energy and solar energy.

solar energy – energy from the sun that can be used for heating and generating electricity.

software – the written programs used to operate a computer.

talc – a very soft mineral that has a soapy feel.

thrive – to do well.

typical – usual or normal.

unique (yoo-NEEK) – being the only one of its kind.